Accounting for Software

Steven M. Bragg

AccountingTools®

Table of Contents

Accounting for Software 1

Introduction *1*

Internal-Use Software *1*

Internal-Use Software Accessed via a Hosting Arrangement *5*

Website Development Costs *6*

Software Intended for Sale *7*
    Initial Cost Recognition 7
    Subsequent Cost Measurement 9
    Product Enhancements 10

Software Inventory *10*

Accounting for Costs to Develop Entertainment and Educational Software *10*

Revenue Recognition for Software Sales *10*
    Step One: Link Contract to Customer 11
    Step Two: Note Performance Obligations 11
    Step Three: Determine Prices 12
    Step Four: Allocate Prices to Obligations 15
    Step Five: Recognize Revenue 17
        Measurement of Progress Completion 17
        Output Methods 17
        Input Methods 18

Presentation Issues *18*

Disclosure Issues *18*

Summary *20*

Glossary **21**

Index **23**

About the Author

Steven Bragg, CPA, has been the chief financial officer or controller of four companies, as well as a consulting manager at Ernst & Young. He received a master's degree in finance from Bentley College, an MBA from Babson College, and a Bachelor's degree in Economics from the University of Maine. He has been a two-time president of the Colorado Mountain Club, and is an avid alpine skier, mountain biker, and certified master diver. Mr. Bragg resides in Centennial, Colorado. He has written more than 300 books and courses, including *New Controller Guidebook*, *GAAP Guidebook*, and *Payroll Management*.

Steven maintains the accountingtools.com web site, which contains continuing professional education courses, the Accounting Best Practices podcast, and thousands of articles on accounting subjects.

Buy Additional AccountingTools Courses

AccountingTools offers more than 1,500 hours of CPE courses, with concentrations in accounting, auditing, finance, taxation, and ethics. Related courses that you might like include:

- Accountants' Guidebook
- Project Accounting
- Project Management

Go to accountingtools.com/cpe to view these additional courses.

AccountingTools®

Accounting for Software

Introduction

The accounting standards relating to software are included in two sections of the GAAP codification. Section 350 covers internal-use software and website development costs, while Section 985 covers software that is intended for sale. In this booklet, we cover the accounting for both scenarios, as well as software accessed via a hosting arrangement, software inventory, software revenue recognition, and related presentation and disclosure topics.

> **Related Podcast Episode:** Episode 270 of the Accounting Best Practices Podcast discusses the accounting for software as a service. It is available at: **accounting-tools.com/podcasts** or **iTunes**

Internal-Use Software

Companies routinely develop software for internal use, and want to understand how these development costs are to be accounted for. Software is considered to be for internal use when it has been acquired or developed *only* for the internal needs of a business. Examples of situations where software is considered to be developed for internal use are:

- Accounting systems
- Cash management tracking systems
- Customer service software
- Data collection and analysis systems
- Database search tools
- Membership tracking systems
- Production automation systems
- Video production systems

Further, there can be no reasonably possible plan to market the software outside of the company, as would be the case when a marketing channel has been selected that has specifically-identified promotional, delivery, billing, and support activities. A market feasibility study is not considered a reasonably possible marketing plan, nor is an arrangement that provides for the joint development of software for mutual internal use. However, a history of selling software that had initially been developed for internal use creates a reasonable assumption that the latest internal-use product will also be marketed for sale outside of the company.

EXAMPLE

Harrison Manufacturing develops just-in-time software that it uses internally to monitor the flow of jobs through its production process. The IT manager convinces management to sell the JIT software outside the company, which meets with some success. Subsequently, the firm develops warehouse management software to manage the flow of goods through its own distribution warehouses. Since Harrison has a history of selling its internally-developed software outside of the firm, there is a reasonable assumption that the same action will be taken for the new warehouse management software – which prevents the firm from accounting for it as internal-use software. Instead, it must account for the new software using the requirements for software that is intended for sale.

EXAMPLE

Inouye Semiconductor uses highly-complex wafer testing software to determine whether the semiconductor chips it is producing are operational. This is internal-use software, since customers do not acquire the software, nor do they obtain the future right to use it.

If the preceding criteria are present, then the entity can begin capitalizing the cost of software development when both of the following conditions are met:

- Management has authorized and committed funding to the software project; and
- It is probable that the project will be completed and the software will perform its intended function.

The capitalization of costs may be temporarily prohibited when there is significant development uncertainty. This situation arises when:

- A project includes novel or unproven features, and the associated uncertainties have not been resolved through coding and testing; or
- The software's significant performance requirements have not been finalized or continue to be substantially revised.

In the preceding situation, development costs must be charged to expense until the uncertainty is eliminated (after which the capitalization of costs can resume). This approach to cost capitalization keeps an organization from capitalizing the cost of a project that is not stable or technically feasible.

EXAMPLE

A software company begins developing an AI-driven tax compliance platform that is intended to interpret newly issued FASB and IRS guidance in real time. The product architecture includes a novel machine-learning engine that has not yet been successfully integrated with the rules-based calculation module. During early development, repeated testing reveals that the engine produces inconsistent outputs, and the development team continues to revise core performance specifications. Because the significant performance requirements remain unstable and technical feasibility has not been established, the company expenses all related payroll and coding costs. After successful system integration testing demonstrates consistent performance and management formally documents technical feasibility, the capitalization of subsequent development costs begins.

Costs that may be capitalized once the probable-to-complete recognition threshold has been met include only the following items:

- External direct costs of materials and services consumed in developing or obtaining the software.
- Payroll and payroll-related costs of employees directly associated with and devoting time to the software project.
- Interest costs incurred during development.
- Costs to develop or obtain software that allows for access to or conversion of old data by new systems.

Any costs incurred before the probable-to-complete recognition threshold is met shall be expensed as incurred. In addition, the following costs shall be expensed as incurred, regardless of timing:

- Training costs
- Data conversion costs, except for those enabling access to or conversion of old data by new systems
- General and administrative costs
- Maintenance costs

If it is no longer probable that a project will be completed, stop capitalizing the costs associated with it, and conduct impairment testing on the costs already capitalized. The cost at which the asset should then be carried is the lower of its carrying amount or fair value (less costs to sell). Unless there is evidence to the contrary, the usual assumption is that uncompleted software has no fair value. The following are general indicators that software is no longer expected to be completed and placed in service:

- Expenditures are no longer being budgeted or incurred for the software.
- There are programming difficulties that will not be resolved on a timely basis.
- There have been significant cost overruns.
- The costs that have been or will be incurred significantly exceed the cost of competing third-party software, so management intends to stop development and buy the third-party software.
- New technology in the marketplace is driving management to acquire third-party products, rather than completing the internal development project.
- The business unit to which the software relates is either unprofitable or will be discontinued.

EXAMPLE

A healthcare technology company capitalizes $4.2 million of development costs for an internally developed patient analytics platform after establishing technological feasibility. Midway through development, management suspends further funding when programming challenges prevent the system from integrating with electronic medical record platforms. At the same time, a third-party vendor releases a compliant, fully tested solution at a significantly lower total cost. Budgeted expenditures for the internal project are removed from the forecast, and the related business unit is slated for restructuring due to declining margins. Management concludes that completion is no longer probable and stops capitalizing additional costs. An impairment test is performed, and because the unfinished software has no observable fair value, the entire carrying amount is written off to expense.

A business may purchase software for internal use. If the purchase price of this software includes other elements, such as training and maintenance fees, only capitalize that portion of the purchase price that relates to the software itself. When this purchase results in the replacement of older software, any remaining unamortized cost of the older software should be charged to expense as soon as the replacement software is ready for its intended use.

In addition, any later upgrades of the software can be capitalized, but only if it is probable that extra system functionality will result from the upgrade. The costs of maintaining the system should be charged to expense as incurred. If the maintenance is provided by a third party and payment is made in advance for the services of that party, amortize the cost of the maintenance over the service period.

Note: When it is not possible to separate internal costs on a cost-effective basis between maintenance and relatively minor upgrades, you should expense these costs as incurred.

Once costs have been capitalized, amortize them over the expected useful life of the software. This is typically done on a straight-line basis, unless another method more clearly reflects the expected usage pattern of the software. Amortization should begin when a software module is ready for its intended use, which is considered to be when all substantial system testing has been completed. If a software module cannot function unless other modules are also completed, do not begin amortization until the related modules are complete.

It may be necessary to regularly reassess the useful life of the software for amortization purposes, since technological obsolescence tends to shorten it. The reassessment may also involve consideration of new technology, competing products, and other economic factors.

The capitalized cost of internal-use software should be routinely reviewed for impairment. The following are all indicators of the possible presence of asset impairment:

- The software is not expected to be of substantive use
- The manner in which the software was originally intended to be used has now changed
- The software is to be significantly altered
- The development cost of the software significantly exceeded original expectations

---

EXAMPLE

A regional bank capitalizes $3 million for internally developed loan origination software after it is placed in service. Two years later, management adopts a new digital strategy that emphasizes cloud-based automation and artificial intelligence tools, rendering the existing platform largely redundant. Loan officers bypass key modules, and planned system enhancements would require a substantial architectural rewrite. In addition, the original project had already exceeded its approved budget by 40 percent. Because the software is no longer expected to provide substantive use in its original configuration and would require significant alteration to remain viable, management performs an impairment analysis. The recoverable amount is determined to be below the carrying value, resulting in a partial write-down of the capitalized asset.

Once a business has developed software for internal use, management may decide to market it for external use by third parties. If so, the proceeds from software licensing, net of selling costs, should be applied against the carrying amount of the software asset. For the purposes of this topic, selling costs are considered to include commissions, software reproduction costs, servicing obligations, warranty costs, and installation costs. The business should not recognize a profit on sales of the software until the application of net sales to the carrying amount of the software asset have reduced the carrying amount to zero. The business can recognize all further proceeds as revenue.

Internal-Use Software Accessed via a Hosting Arrangement

The guidance noted in the preceding section also applies to the fees paid by a customer in a cloud computing arrangement (where software and/or data are being hosted on the systems of a third party). In this situation, capitalized implementation costs are ratably charged to expense over the term of the hosting arrangement. The term of a hosting arrangement is considered to be its fixed non-cancellable term, plus any option extension periods, if the company is reasonably certain to exercise the option. The term of the arrangement should be periodically reassessed, with any changes in the period accounted for as a change in accounting estimate.

> **Note:** Capitalization begins only when management has authorized and committed to funding the implementation, it is probable that the implementation will be completed and used as intended, and significant development uncertainty does not exist.

Under a hosting arrangement, it is relatively common for the price to include several elements, such as the software license, hosting, and employee training. When this is the case, the company should allocate the price paid among these various elements, where the allocation is based on the standalone price of each element in the contract.

The accountant should examine the capitalized costs associated with a hosting arrangement for impairment when any of the following conditions are present:

- The arrangement is not expected to provide any substantive service potential to the company.
- A significant change has occurred in the extent to which the hosting arrangement is used.
- A significant change has been made to the hosting arrangement.

Website Development Costs

A company may allocate funds to the development of a company website, in such areas as coding, graphics design, the addition of content, and site operation. The accounting for website development is identical to the accounting just described for internal-use software.

The accounting treatment is as follows:

- Costs to develop website functionality and underlying software are evaluated for capitalization under the internal-use software model.
- Costs to obtain and register an internet domain are evaluated for capitalization under intangible asset guidance.
- Costs to develop initial graphics are evaluated under the internal-use software model.
- Costs to input website content are expensed as incurred.
- Website hosting fees are expensed over the period benefited.
- Costs to register the website with search engines are expensed as incurred, since they are advertising costs.

EXAMPLE

Greenfield Equipment decides to launch a new corporate website to provide product specifications, dealer locations, and online warranty registration. On March 1, management approves funding and concludes that the website's significant performance requirements are defined and that no novel or unproven functionality exists. Accordingly, capitalization begins on that date. Fees paid to a third-party developer to build the site architecture and customer portal are capitalized, as are the payroll costs of internal IT staff directly coding the system. The cost to register the domain name is evaluated for capitalization as an intangible asset. Graphic design costs for the site layout are capitalized. By contrast, costs to upload product descriptions and photographs are expensed, as are search engine registration fees. Monthly hosting fees are expensed over the service period.

Software Intended for Sale

When computer software is to be sold, leased, or otherwise marketed for sale, there are a number of accounting requirements for how the associated costs are to be treated. Examples of software intended for sale are as follows:

- Software that is required to operate a company's products
- Machines that are sold with software incorporated into them that is needed to operate the machines
- Vehicles that are sold with automated driving systems installed in them
- A database that is sold with an integrated software search function
- An operating system that is installed on computers sold to customers

The accounting requirements for software intended for sale are noted in the following sub-sections.

Initial Cost Recognition

The following requirements apply to the initial recognition of various costs associated with computer software that is intended for sale:

- *Research and development costs.* Any cost incurred to establish the technological feasibility of software is to be charged to expense as incurred. Technological feasibility has been established when the developing entity has completed all planning, designing, coding and testing activities required to determine whether the software can meet its design specifications. Evidence of technological feasibility can be proven by engaging in either of the following activities:

o *Detail program design option.* If a detail program design was developed for the software, then all three of the following requirements must be met in order to establish technological feasibility:

1. The needed skills, hardware, and software technology are available to produce the product.
2. The detail program design is sufficiently complete, based on design documentation and by tracing the design to product specifications.
3. The detail program design has been examined for high-risk development issues and these concerns have been resolved with coding and testing. Examples of high-risk development issues are unproven functions and features that incorporate technological innovations.

> **Note:** When a high-risk development issue is discovered after technological feasibility was established and costs capitalized, this is considered a change in accounting estimate that requires all previously capitalized costs to be charged to expense.

> **Note:** When software does not include all of the features originally planned for it and the product is not sellable without the dropped features, then technological feasibility has not been established for it.

o *No detail program design.* When there is no detail program design, then technological feasibility can be proven by having a completed product design and a working model of the software, where the completeness of the model and its consistency with the product design have been confirmed with sufficient testing. A working model must be operative, written in the same language as the product to be sold, include all planned major functions, and be ready for initial customer testing.

> **Note:** When a product consists of several modules that cannot be sold separately, technological feasibility must be established for the product as a whole, rather than on a module-by-module basis. This means that the detail program design or the working model for the entire product must be completed before capitalization can begin.

- *Production costs.* The recognition of production costs is addressed in the following topics:

  o *Production masters.* Once technological feasibility has been established, the cost of producing production masters should be capitalized. These costs may include any coding and testing conducted after technological feasibility was established.

- o *Software production costs*. Software production costs cannot be capitalized until technological feasibility has been established, and all research and development activities for the other components of the product have been completed.
- o *Allocated overhead costs*. Overhead costs can be allocated to production. This allocation may include overhead relating to programmers and their work facilities, but should not include an allocation of general and administrative costs.
- o *Capitalization stoppage*. The capitalization of production costs must stop when the product is available for general release to customers.
- o *Maintenance and customer support costs*. The costs of maintenance and customer support should be charged to expense at the earlier of when these costs are incurred or when related revenue is recognized.

- *Purchased software*. When software is purchased in order to be integrated into a product, the acquisition cost should only be capitalized if technological feasibility can be established *and* all research and development activities of the other components of the product have been completed as of the software purchase date. If there is an alternative use for the purchased software, then the purchase cost can be capitalized in accordance with its projected use.

EXAMPLE

Norrona Software buys software for $50,000 that it can resell for $40,000. Technological feasibility has not yet been established. At this point, $10,000 of the purchase cost should be charged to research and development expense, while the remaining $40,000 is capitalized. The technological feasibility of the software product is then established, so Norrona can include the capitalized $40,000 in the cost of the product.

Subsequent Cost Measurement

Once software costs have been capitalized, they should be amortized on a product-by-product basis, beginning with the date when the product is available for general release to customers. The amount of annual amortization recognized should be the greater of the following two calculation options:

- The ratio of current gross product revenues to the total of both current and expected future gross revenues for that product; or
- The straight-line method over the remaining estimated economic life of the product.

At the end of each reporting period, compare the unamortized capital costs of each software product to its net realizable value, and write off any amount by which the unamortized capital costs exceed the net realizable value. Net realizable value is the estimated future gross revenues for that product, minus the estimated future costs of completing and disposing of it, which includes any maintenance and customer service costs. Any amounts written off shall not be restored in future periods.

Product Enhancements

Enhancements may be made to a product after it has been initially released for sale. The costs incurred for these enhancements should be charged to research and development expense until such time as the technological feasibility of each enhancement has been established. Technological feasibility tends to be easier to establish for a product enhancement, since it was already established for the baseline product. This is particularly the case when a software product has been ported (adapted) to run on different hardware.

If the original product (prior to the enhanced version), will no longer be sold, then include any unamortized cost of the original version in the cost of the enhancement when applying the net realizable value test. However, if the original product will continue to be sold along with the enhanced version, then allocate the unamortized cost of the original product between the original and enhanced versions.

The capitalized costs of a product enhancement, including any costs allocated to it from the original product, should be amortized over the estimated useful life of the enhanced product.

Software Inventory

When a software provider incurs costs to duplicate software, documentation, and training materials from product masters, as well as to package these items, the costs should be capitalized as inventory. These capitalized costs are then charged to the cost of goods sold when the revenue associated with the sale of these units is recognized.

Accounting for Costs to Develop Entertainment and Educational Software

The Securities and Exchange Commission (SEC) observer sitting in on an Emerging Issues Task Force meeting has pointed out that the SEC is aware of diversity in the entertainment industry in how software development costs relating to educational and entertainment products are accounted for. The treatment ranges from capitalizing all costs to expensing a significant proportion of them as incurred. The SEC observer pointed out that educational and entertainment products that are sold, leased, or otherwise marketed are subject to the requirements of Topic 985, *Software*. This booklet dealt with Topic 985 in its *Software Intended for Sale* and *Software Inventory* sections.

Revenue Recognition for Software Sales

There used to be a number of revenue recognition rules relating to the sale of software, which were eliminated when Topic 606 of the Accounting Standards Codification, *Revenue from Contracts with Customers*, was implemented. Topic 606 establishes a series of actions that an entity takes to determine the amount and timing of revenue to be recognized. The main steps are:

1. Link the contract with a specific customer.
2. Note the performance obligations required by the contract.
3. Determine the price of the underlying transaction.
4. Match this price to the performance obligations through an allocation process.
5. Recognize revenue as the various obligations are fulfilled.

We will expand upon each of these steps in the following sub-sections, limiting the discussion to those aspects of revenue recognition that are most likely to apply to the sale of software.

Step One: Link Contract to Customer

The contract is used as a central aspect of revenue recognition, because revenue recognition is closely associated with it. In many instances, revenue is recognized at multiple points in time over the duration of a contract, so linking contracts with revenue recognition provides a reasonable framework for establishing the timing and amounts of revenue recognition.

A contract only exists if there is an agreement between the parties that establishes enforceable rights and obligations. It is not necessary for an agreement to be in writing for it to be considered a contract.

Step Two: Note Performance Obligations

A performance obligation is essentially the unit of account for the goods or services contractually promised to a customer. The performance obligations in the contract must be clearly identified. This is important in recognizing revenue, since revenue is considered to be recognizable when goods or services are transferred to the customer.

If there is more than one good or service to be transferred under the contract terms, only break it out as a separate performance obligation if it is a distinct obligation or there are a series of transfers to the customer of a distinct good or service. In the latter case, a separate performance obligation is assumed if there is a consistent pattern of transfer to the customer.

The "distinct" label can be applied to a good or service only if it meets both of the following criteria:

- *Capable of being distinct.* The customer can benefit from the good or service as delivered, or in combination with other resources that the customer can readily find; and
- *Distinct within the context of the contract.* The promised delivery of the good or service is separately identified within the contract.

Goods or services are more likely to be considered distinct when:

- The seller does not use the goods or services as a component of an integrated bundle of goods or services.
- The items do not significantly modify any other goods or services listed in the contract.
- The items are not highly interrelated with other goods or services listed in the contract.

The intent of these evaluative factors is to place a focus on how to determine whether goods or services are truly distinct within a contract. There is no need to assess the customer's intended use of any goods or services when making this determination.

To reduce the cost of noting performance obligations, it is not necessary to assess whether promised goods or services are performance obligations if they are immaterial in the context of the contract with the customer.

EXAMPLE

Norrona Software enters into a contract with a Scandinavian clothing manufacturer to transfer a software license for its clothing design software. The contract also states that Norrona will install the software and provide technical support for a two-year period. The installation process involves adjusting the data entry screens to match the needs of the clothing designers who will use the software. The software can be used without these installation changes. The technical support assistance is intended to provide advice to users regarding advanced features, and is not considered a key requirement for software users.

Since the software is functional without the installation process or the technical support, Norrona concludes that the items are not highly interrelated. Since these goods and services are distinct, the company should identify separate performance obligations for the software license, installation work, and technical support.

In the event that a good or service is not classified as distinct, aggregate it with other goods or services promised in the contract, until such time as a cluster of goods or services have been accumulated that can be considered distinct.

Step Three: Determine Prices

This step involves the determination of the transaction price built into the contract. The transaction price is the amount of consideration to be paid by the customer in exchange for its receipt of goods or services. The transaction price does not include any amounts collected on behalf of third parties (such as sales taxes).

EXAMPLE

The Productivity Software Company sells its software to individuals through its chain of retail stores. In the most recent period, the company generated $3,800,000 of receipts, of which $200,000 was sales taxes collected on behalf of local governments. Since the $200,000 was collected on behalf of third parties, it cannot be recognized as revenue.

If the transaction price is to be paid over a period of time (as may be the case with a large software sale), this implies that the seller is including a financing component in the contract. If this financing component is a significant financing benefit for the customer and provides financing for more than one year, adjust the transaction price for the time value of money. In cases where there is a financing component to a contract, the seller will earn interest income over the term of the contract.

A contract may contain a financing component, even if there is no explicit reference to it in the contract. When adjusting the transaction price for the time value of money, consider the following factors:

- *Standalone price.* The amount of revenue recognized should reflect the price that a customer would have paid if it had paid in cash.
- *Significance.* In order to be recognized, the financing component should be significant. This means evaluating the amount of the difference between the consideration to be paid and the cash selling price. Also note the combined effect of prevailing interest rates and the time difference between when delivery is made and when the customer pays.

If it is necessary to adjust the compensation paid for the time value of money, use as a discount rate the rate that would be employed in a separate financing transaction between the parties as of the beginning date of the contract. The rate used should reflect the credit characteristics of the customer, including the presence of any collateral provided. This discount rate is not to be updated after the commencement of the contract, irrespective of any changes in the credit markets or in the credit standing of the customer.

EXAMPLE

Norrona Software sells one license for enterprise resources planning software to Eskimo Construction, under generous terms that allow Eskimo to pay Norrona the full amount of the $119,990 receivable in 24 months. The cash selling price of the software is $105,000. The contract contains an implicit interest rate of 6.9%, which is the interest rate that discounts the purchase price of $119,990 down to the cash selling price over the two-year period. The controller examines this rate and concludes that it approximates the rate that Norrona and Eskimo would use if there had been a separate financing transaction between them as of the contract inception date. Consequently, Norrona recognizes interest income during the two-year period prior to the payment due date, using the following calculation:

Year	Beginning Balance	Interest (at 6.9% Rate)	Ending Balance
1	$105,000	$7,245	$112,245
2	112,245	7,745	$119,990

As of the shipment date, Norrona records the following entry:

	Debit	Credit
Loan receivable	105,000	
Revenue		105,000

At the end of the first year, Norrona recognizes the interest associated with the transaction for the first year, using the following entry:

	Debit	Credit
Loan receivable	7,245	
Interest income		7,245

At the end of the second year, Norrona recognizes the interest associated with the transaction for the second year, using the following entry:

	Debit	Credit
Loan receivable	7,745	
Interest income		7,745

These entries increase the size of the loan receivable until it reaches the original sale price of $119,990. Eskimo then pays the full amount of the receivable, at which point Norrona records the following final entry:

	Debit	Credit
Cash	119,990	
Loan receivable		119,990

There is assumed *not* to be a significant financing component to a contract in the presence of any of the following factors:

- *Advance payment.* The customer paid in advance, and the customer can specify when goods and services are to be delivered.
- *Variable component.* A large part of the consideration to be paid is variable, and payment timing will vary based on a future event that is not under the control of either party.

- *Non-financing reason.* The reason for the difference between the contractual consideration and the cash selling price exists for a reason other than financing, and the amount of the difference is proportional to the alternative reason.

Step Four: Allocate Prices to Obligations

Once the performance obligations and transaction prices associated with a contract have been identified, the next step is to allocate the transaction prices to the obligations. The basic rule is to allocate that price to a performance obligation that best reflects that amount of consideration to which the seller expects to be entitled when it satisfies each performance obligation. To determine this allocation, it is first necessary to estimate the standalone selling price of those distinct goods or services as of the inception date of the contract. If it is not possible to derive a standalone selling price, the seller must estimate it. This estimation should involve all relevant information that is reasonably available, such as:

- Competitive pressure on prices
- Costs incurred to manufacture or provide the item
- Item profit margins
- Pricing of other items in the same contract
- Standalone selling price of the item
- Supply and demand for the items in the market
- The seller's pricing strategy and practices
- The type of customer, distribution channel, or geographic region
- Third-party pricing

The following three approaches are acceptable ways in which to estimate a standalone selling price:

- *Adjusted market assessment.* This involves reviewing the market to estimate the price at which a customer in that market would be willing to pay for the goods and services in question. This can involve an examination of the prices of competitors for similar items and adjusting them to incorporate the seller's costs and margins.
- *Expected cost plus a margin.* This requires the seller to estimate the costs required to fulfill a performance obligation, and then add a margin to it to derive the estimated price.
- *Residual approach.* This involves subtracting all of the observable standalone selling prices from the total transaction price to arrive at the residual price remaining for allocation to any non-observable selling prices. This method can only be used if one of the following situations applies:
  - The seller sells the good or service to other customers for a wide range of prices; or
  - No price has yet been established for that item, and it has not yet been sold on a standalone basis.

The residual approach can be difficult to use when there are several goods or services with uncertain standalone selling prices. If so, it may be necessary to use a combination of methods to derive standalone selling prices, which should be used in the following order:

1. Estimate the aggregate amount of the standalone selling prices for all items having uncertain standalone selling prices, using the residual method.
2. Use another method to develop standalone selling prices for each item in this group, to allocate the aggregate amount of the standalone selling prices.

Once all standalone selling prices have been determined, allocate the transaction price amongst these distinct goods or services based on their relative standalone selling prices.

Tip: Appropriate evidence of a standalone selling price is the observable price of a good or service when the seller sells it to a similar customer under similar circumstances.

Once the seller derives an approach for estimating a standalone selling price, it should consistently apply that method to the derivation of the standalone selling prices for other goods or services with similar characteristics.

EXAMPLE

Disaster Recovery Corporation produces apps for the iPhone. The company receives an order from the federal government for 50,000 units of its hurricane preparedness app, as well as for 10,000 units of a new app that sends out alerts when tornadoes are nearby. The company has not yet sold the new tornado app to anyone. The total price of the order is $600,000. The company assigns $450,000 of the total price to the hurricane preparedness app, based on its own sales of comparable orders. This leaves $150,000 of the total price that is allocable to the tornado app. Since the company has not yet established a price for this app and has not sold it on a standalone basis, it is acceptable to allocate $150,000 to the tornado app under the residual approach.

If there is a subsequent change in the transaction price, allocate that change amongst the distinct goods or services based on the original allocation that was used at the inception of the contract. If this subsequent allocation is to a performance obligation that has already been completed and for which revenue has already been recognized, the result can be an increase or reduction in the amount of revenue recognized. This change in recognition should occur as soon as the subsequent change in the transaction price occurs.

Step Five: Recognize Revenue

Revenue is to be recognized as goods or services are transferred to the customer. This transference is considered to occur when the customer gains control over the good or service. Indicators of this date include the following:

- When the seller has the right to receive payment.
- When the customer has legal title to the transferred asset. This can still be the case even when the seller retains title to protect it against the customer's failure to pay.
- When physical possession of the asset has been transferred by the seller.
- When the customer has taken on the significant risks and rewards of ownership related to the asset transferred by the seller. For example, the customer can now sell, pledge, or exchange the asset.
- When the customer accepts the asset.
- When the customer can prevent other entities from using or obtaining benefits from the asset.

Measurement of Progress Completion

When a performance obligation is being completed over a period of time, the seller recognizes revenue through the application of a progress completion method. The goal of this method is to determine the progress of the seller in achieving complete satisfaction of its performance obligation. This method is to be consistently applied over time, and shall be re-measured at the end of each reporting period.

Both output methods and input methods are considered acceptable for determining progress completion. The method chosen should incorporate due consideration of the nature of the goods or services being provided to the customer. The following subsections address the use of output and input methods.

Output Methods

An output method recognizes revenue based on a comparison of the value to the customer of goods and services transferred to date to the remaining goods and services not yet transferred. There are numerous ways to measure output, including:

- Surveys of performance to date
- Milestones reached
- The passage of time
- The number of units delivered
- The number of units produced

Another output method that may be acceptable is the amount of consideration that the seller has the right to invoice, such as billable hours. This approach works when the seller has a right to invoice an amount that matches the amount of performance completed to date.

Input Methods

An input method derives the amount of revenue to be recognized based on the to-date effort required by the seller to satisfy a performance obligation relative to the total estimated amount of effort required. Examples of possible inputs are costs incurred and labor hours expended.

A method based on output is preferred, since it most faithfully depicts the performance of the seller under the terms of a contract. However, an input-based method is certainly allowable if using it would be less costly for the seller, while still providing a reasonable proxy for the ongoing measurement of progress.

Presentation Issues

The following issues relate to the presentation of information for capitalized costs related to a software hosting arrangement:

- *Amortization classification*. The amortization expense for capitalized costs for a hosting arrangement should be included in the same line item on the income statement as the expense for fees associated with the hosting arrangement.
- *Balance sheet presentation*. The capitalized implementation costs for a hosting arrangement should be included in the same line item as the prepayment of hosting fees.
- *Statement of cash flows presentation*. The cash flows from capitalized implementation costs should be classified in the same manner as the cash flows for the associated hosting fees.

The following issues relate to the presentation of information for software that is intended for sale:

- *Amortization classification*. The amortization expense for software should be charged to the cost of sales on the income statement.
- *Balance sheet presentation*. Present capitalized software costs with a life of more than one year in the other asset line item.

Disclosure Issues

The disclosures that accompany the financial statements should include the following items:

- Unamortized software costs
- The amount charged to expense for software amortization
- The software amount written down to net realizable value
- The nature of any hosting arrangements that are service contracts

SAMPLE DISCLOSURE

Research and development expenses consist primarily of salary and related expenses, including stock-based compensation, for personnel related to the development of improvements and expanded features for our services, as well as quality assurance, testing, product management and allocated overhead. Research and development costs are expensed as incurred except for internal use software development costs that qualify for capitalization. The Company reviews development costs incurred for internal-use software in the application development stage and assesses costs for capitalization.

SAMPLE DISCLOSURE

The Company capitalizes software development costs incurred in connection with the localization and translation of its products once technological feasibility has been achieved based on a working model. A working model is defined as an operative version of the computer software product that is completed in the same software language as the product to be ultimately marketed, performs all the major functions planned for the product and is ready for initial customer testing (usually identified as beta testing). In addition, the Company capitalizes software purchased from third parties or through business combinations as acquired software technology, if the related software under development has reached technological feasibility.

The amortization of capitalized software costs is the greater of the straight-line basis over three years, the expected useful life, or a computation using a ratio of current revenue for a product compared to the estimated total of current and future revenues for that product. The Company periodically compares the unamortized capitalized software costs to the estimated net realizable value of the associated product. The amount by which the unamortized capitalized software costs of a particular software product exceeds the estimated net realizable value of that asset would be reported as a charge to the Consolidated Statements of Operations and Comprehensive Income (Loss). Capitalized software costs and accumulated amortization at January 31 were as follows:

(000s)	20X2	20X1
Capitalized software costs:		
Capitalized software development costs	$2,314	$1,516
Acquired software technology	135	--
	2,449	1,516
Less accumulated amortization	-851	-526
Capitalized software costs, net	$1,598	$990

It is the Company's policy to write off capitalized software development costs once fully amortized. Accordingly, during fiscal 20X2, $0.3 million of costs and accumulated amortization was removed from the Consolidated Balance Sheet and was primarily related to acquired software technology which was fully amortized during fiscal 20X2. Amortization of capitalized software costs is included in "Cost of license fees" in the accompanying Consolidated Statements of Operations and Comprehensive Income. The following table summarizes the estimated amortization expense relating to the Company's capitalized software costs as of January 31, 20X2:

Fiscal Years	(000s)
20X3	$759
20X4	572
20X5	226
20X6	27
Thereafter	<u>14</u>
	<u>$1,598</u>

Summary

The accounting rules are significantly different for internal-use software and software intended for sale, so there should be clear internal guidelines for how to identify each situation. Impairment is also a significant concern, since software can be rendered technologically obsolete in short order; this means that the accounting staff must continually monitor the circumstances to see if an impairment analysis is warranted. Finally, the abbreviated revenue recognition rules noted in this booklet should apply to most software sales; for a more complete treatment of the topic, see the author's *Revenue Recognition* course.

Glossary

C

Coding. Detailed instructions in a computer language to enact the requirements stated in the associated detail program design.

D

Detail program design. The detailed specifications of a computer software product that takes product functions, features, and technical requirements to their most detailed form.

H

Hosting arrangement. An arrangement in which the end user of software does not take possession of it; instead, the software resides on the supplier's or a third party's hardware, where the customer accesses it.

M

Maintenance. Those actions taken after a product is available for general release, to correct errors or update the product with more current information.

P

Preliminary project stage. A stage during the development of software when performance requirements are determined, alternatives are explored, and technology feasibility studies are conducted, along with several related activities.

Product design. The logical representation of all product functions in enough detail to serve as product specifications.

Product enhancement. Improvements made to an existing product that are intended to prolong its life or significantly enhance its marketability. Product enhancements usually call for a redesign of all or part of an existing product.

Product master. A completed version of a software product that is ready for copying.

S

Software. A set of programs that interact with each other, causing a computer to perform work.

T

Testing. The performance of those steps needed to determine whether software meets the function, feature, and technical performance requirements stated in the product design.

W

Working model. An operational version of software that performs all major functions planned for it, and which is ready for initial customer testing.

Index

Adjusted market assessment................. 15

Contracts, linkage to customers........... 11

Disclosure issues 18
Discount rate....................................... 13
Distinct criterion................................. 11

Expected cost plus a margin 15

Input methods 18

Output methods 17

Performance obligations....................... 11
Presentation issues............................... 18

Price allocations 15
Price determination 12
Progress completion method................. 17

Residual approach................................. 16
Revenue recognition 17
    Steps.. 10

Software
    Intended for sale................................. 7
    Internal-use 1
    Inventory.. 10
    Product enhancements...................... 10

Time value of money 13

Website development costs..................... 6

www.ingramcontent.com/pod-product-compliance
Lightning Source LLC
Chambersburg PA
CBHW051430200326
41520CB00023B/7427